Marine Life For Young Readers

Starfish & Urchins

Contents

Text by Stanley L. Swartz
Photography by Robert Yin

DOMINIE PRESS
Pearson Learning Group

About Starfish

Starfish live in the sea and look like **stars**. They are also called sea stars. They move very slowly. It takes them a long time to go from one place to another.

◀ **Red Starfish**

Where Starfish Live

There are many different types of starfish. Some have long arms and some have short arms. Some live on the ocean floor. Some live around **coral reefs**.

◄ Knobby Starfish

What Starfish Look Like

Starfish are covered with small **spines**. The spines are sharp and pointed. Starfish like to eat oysters and clams. The mouth of a starfish is on the bottom of its body.

◀ **Crown-of-Thorns Starfish**

Most starfish have five arms. There is an **eye** on the end of each arm. The eye sees only light and darkness. If a starfish loses an arm, it can grow a new one.

◀ **Red Starfish**

Starfish have feet that look like **tubes**. The tube feet help them move. They have hundreds of feet. These feet also help them get food.

◄ **Brittle Starfish**

Starfish come in many colors. The most **common** colors are yellow, red, orange, and pink. Some starfish are only one color and some are many colors. The different colors help protect them.

◀ **Feather Star**

About Urchins

Urchins have a hard **shell**. Some urchins live in warm water and some live in cold water. They are also called sea urchins. There are more than 800 kinds of urchins.

◄ **Red Sea Urchin**

Where Urchins Live

Urchins can live in shallow water or very deep water. They eat both plants and animals. They eat with a **jaw** that has sharp teeth. This jaw is on the bottom of the urchin's body.

◄ **Black Sea Urchin**

What Urchins Look Like

Urchins are **covered** with spines. Some spines are long and some are short. Their spines help them move. They are slow movers.

◄ Pencil Urchin

Some urchins have hundreds of spines. The spines come in many colors. They are used for protection. Some of these spines are **poisonous**.

◄ **White Sea Urchin**

Urchins **creep** along the sea bottom. They also creep around coral reefs. Urchins come in many sizes and shapes. They can be as small as a pea or as large as your fist.

◄ **Striped Sea Urchin**

Glossary

common:	Usual; well-known
coral reefs:	Hard shelves of coral
covered:	Protected, hidden, sheltered, or concealed
creep:	To move slowly
eye:	Something that is used to see
jaw:	The part of the mouth used to bite and chew
poisonous:	Something that can make you ill or kill you
shell:	A hard cover
spines:	Long needle-like points growing out of an animal or plant
stars:	Shapes with five or more points
tubes:	Shapes that are round and hollow

Index